# Crossroads Mamas' 105 Spiritual Baths for Every Occasion

## Quickly & Easily Improve your Quality of Life with Spiritual and Magical Baths

By Denise Alvarado and
Madrina Angelique

First published in 2012 by Creole Moon Publications

ISBN-10: 1479106232 (paper)
EAN-13: 978-1479106233 (paper)

Primary Category: Body, Mind & Spirit/ Magick Studies
Country of Publication: United States
Publication Date: 8th Moon, 2012
Language: English

Library of Congress Cataloging-in-Publication Data pending


Cover design by Denise Alvarado
Cover © Denise Alvarado
Interior by Denise Alvarado

Typeset in Georgia with Impact and Arial

Disclaimer: The information in this book is for educational purposes only. The information has not been evaluated by the Food and Drug Administration and is not intended to diagnose, treat, cure, or prevent any disease.

# TABLE OF CONTENTS

creolemoonpublications.org

# Crossroads Mamas' 105 Spiritual Baths for Every Occasion

## Quickly & Easily Improve your Quality of Life with Spiritual and Magical Baths

By Denise Alvarado and
Madrina Angelique

# Why Spiritual Baths?

What's not to like about a relaxing aromatic bath? How about a wonderfully fragrant bath with the power to draw in business, bring good luck, create a sense of wellbeing, wash off evil and negative energies and help you succeed in life?

That is the nature of spiritual bathing. An ancient and restorative practice that promotes health and wellbeing, spiritual baths combine the healing power of water with various herbs and minerals to shift spiritual energy in your favor. Rootworkers, Hoodoos, and conjurers of all varieties have long looked to the healing and supernatural qualities of spiritual baths to improve quality of life and to influence self, others, conditions and the environment.

Spiritual bathing is found in many cultures all over the world. In the African-derived traditions such as Santería and Hoodoo, spiritual baths are often prescribed for specific purposes such as drawing love and money, facilitating healing, cultivating wisdom, removing negative conditions, uncrossing and reversing spiritual attacks, providing protection, increasing personal influence and domination and creating success. Sometimes used bathwater is saved and utilized in further works. This book contains special baths for all of these purposes.

At times, holy water is added to spiritual baths. Almost always the spiritual bath itself is blessed. Holy and blessed water are used among the major religions of the world as well for some of the same reasons as is found in folk magic. For protection from the "powers of darkness" for example, the Catholic Church specifically refers to the use of holy water. Holy water is believed to have the power to exorcise evil spirits and cleanse an environment of spiritual impurities. It is used as a sacrament in blessings, exorcisms and baptisms.

Across the globe, cultures share similar beliefs regarding the sanctity of natural bodies of water, waterfalls, and rainfall. For example, in the Middle Ages holy water was often stolen by practitioners of witchcraft. Because of the irrational fear of what would be done with it, holy water was held under lock and key. In Ancient Greek religion, holy water was used for purifying people, places and things. In some magical traditions such as Wicca and Hoodoo, holy water or blessed water is created by adding ordinary table salt to water while praying or chanting. It is then used in many ceremonies and rituals.

The formulas for the baths in this book come from a variety of sources. Drawing from Santería, New Orleans Voodoo, and Hoodoo traditions, each bath is laden with meaning and holds the power of the tradition from which it derives. Some of the baths are based on the conjure oil formulas of the same name, and some of them are based on baths described by informants in Harry Middleton Hyatt's seminal work, *Hoodoo Conjuration, Witchcraft and Rootwork*. Many of the bath recipes come from the authors' own personal formularies.

# Taking a Spiritual Bath: Step-by-Step

There are many ways to take a spiritual bath. How one is taken depends largely upon the purpose of the bath. Some are taken on certain days of the week during certain moon phases or time of day. While these specifics make for amplifying the bath's effects, any of the baths in this book can be taken at any time if an urgent need arises.

There are two methods for taking spiritual baths. One is full immersion and the other is pouring the prepared bath over one's head while standing. Regardless of the method used, the results are the same.

Here are some basic guidelines for taking a spiritual bath – follow these guidelines if there are no specifics given.

1. To prepare an herbal bath, place herbs into a pot of boiling water and let them steep for three to nine minutes. Strain out the herbs and add the liquid tea to your bath.

2. Baths for drawing things to you such as love, success, luck and healing, work well when taken at or before dawn. Wake up before dawn and draw your water. Fill the tub with warm water and wash your body in an upward direction. If possible and you are so inclined, you can take baths for drawing things during a waxing or full moon.

3. For uncrossing baths or getting rid of negative energies and conditions like anger or anxiety, take your bath at sunset and wash your body in a downward motion. Pour the water over your head 9 times so that the water runs down your body while you are standing. If possible and you are so inclined, you can take baths for removing negative energies and conditions during a waning moon.

4. Always bless the water before getting into the tub. You can do this through prayer or invocation of the spirits, saints, and orishas of the healing waters in a manner that is meaningful to you. Alternately, you can use a more general type of blessing. See the water blessings in the next section for examples.

5. Spend at least fifteen minutes soaking in the healing water for a ritual bath. You may

meditate, visualize a resolution of your problem, pray, sing, sit or lay in silence. Do whatever feels comforting to you unless otherwise specified for a particular condition.

6. Save all or a portion of the bathwater for proper disposal. Some common ways of disposing bathwater include tossing it towards the east during sunrise or leaving it at a crossroads.

7. Always clean your tub with saltwater afterwards. Sea salt is best, though regular salt will also do, so long as you have prayed over it. Also, be sure to clean any objects used in the tub with saltwater.

8. As part of preparing your ritual bath, you may light your favorite incense and light a candle in a fitting color to make the experience especially comforting, effective, and enjoyable.

9. Always take a soap bath prior to or after a spiritual bath. Never use soap, oils, or anything else while taking a spiritual bath unless it is specified.

10. Never stay in a spiritual bath longer than thirty minutes.

11. For optimal effect, spiritual baths are taken an odd number of days, from 1 to 13.

12. Allow your body to air dry to achieve the full effect.

13. Always dress in fresh, clean clothes and sleep on clean (preferably white) sheets after taking a spiritual bath.

# Water Blessings

To bless a spiritual bath or to make water holy for use in a spiritual bath, it needs to be consecrated in some fashion. According to some beliefs, water can only be made holy if it is touched by a saint or blessed by someone with a high spiritual consciousness. Some believe water can be made holy by chanting the name of God over it, or by adding blessed salt, holy ash or holy earth to it. Holy earth refers to places where the highest orders of saints have lived. Salt can be blessed by praying the 23rd psalm over it.

There are many ways to bless a spiritual bath. Try one of the methods below, or simply say a heartfelt prayer of your own in the tradition that is most meaningful to you.

## Catholic Water Blessing
*O Lord, Almighty God, who hast given us an ample supply of water, led off by pipes from this source, grant that, by Thy assistance and blessing and our cooperation, every diabolical attack and confusion may be kept off and that this water supply may always be pure and uncontaminated. Through Christ our Lord. Amen.*

## Angel Blessing

*As a child of God, I bless this water that it may
nourish my soul and enrich and heal my body.*


## The Benediction of the Salt

One of the most common ways to make holy water is
by adding blessed salt to the water. To make blessed
salt you can recite the *Benediction of the Salt* as
written in the Holy Bible. First, pour sea salt or
Kosher salt into a clean white bowl and then speak
over the salt the following words:

*The Blessing of the Father Almighty be upon this
Creature of Salt, and let all malignity and hindrance
be cast forth hence from, and let all good enter
herein, for without Thee man cannot live, wherefore
I bless thee and invoke thee, that thou mayest aid
me.*

~Key of Solomon the King, Book II Chapter 5


Then, read Psalm 103 out loud.

Next, procure some water from a natural source.
Sprinkle the blessed salt into the water while reciting
the following biblical passage:

*I exorcise thee, O Creature of Water, by Him Who hath created thee and gathered thee together into one place so that the dry land appeared, that thou uncover all the deceits of the Enemy, and that thou cast out from thee all the impurities and uncleanness of the Spirits of the World of Phantasm, so they may harm me not, through the virtue of God Almighty Who liveth and reigneth unto the Ages of the Ages. Amen.*

~Key of Solomon the King, Book II Chapter 5

# Domination and Coercion Baths

## Bend-over Bath

A gentle commanding bath that makes other people do your bidding. Use to break any hexes and to order evil spirits to return to the place from whence they came.

- Calamus essential oil
- Licorice root
- Bergamot essential oil
- Vetivert essential oil
- Rose geranium essential oil

Add the ingredients to your bathwater. Completely submerge your head 7 times. When done, save some of the bathwater to leave at a crossroads along with 3 pennies.

## Domination Bath

To gain power and influence over anyone and any condition. Simmer the following ingredients on the stove in a gallon of spring water for 9 minutes. Strain and add the water to your bathwater for domination and control. Say the *Domination Prayer to St. Martha* to enhance the effects.

- Patchouli essential oil
- Handful of vetivert
- Lime juice
- Frankincense essential oil
- Calamus root
- Licorice root

## *Domination Prayer*

*St. Martha, I resort to thy aid and protection. Comfort me in all my difficulties and through the great favors thou didst enjoy when the Saviour was lodged in thy house, intercede for my family, that we be provided for in our necessities. I ask of thee, St. Martha, to overcome all difficulties as thou didst overcome the dragon which thou hadst at thy feet. Amen.*

Pray 1 Our Father, 1 Hail Mary, 1 Glory be

# Good Luck Baths

## Attract Good Luck in Everyday Life

To attract and keep good luck, add the following ingredients to a weekly bath.

- Goat's milk
- Sea salt
- Fresh parsley

## Bath for Success and Luck

This is an old New Orleans bath recipe that will keep you in good luck and success.

- Handful of sea salt
- Oil of geranium

Add the ingredients to your bathwater and wash yourself down. Throw the remaining bathwater towards the sun at sunrise.

## Good Luck Gambling Bath

When you want to win at gambling, take this bath before the games begin. Boil for 3 minutes, strain, allow to cool and add to bathwater.

- Holy water
- Spring water
- 1 bunch fresh basil
- 1 bunch fresh rosemary
- 3 gold coins

## Louisiana Van Van Good Luck Bath

Used for good luck and power of all kinds.

- Handful of lemongrass
- Handful of vetivert

Simmer the herbs in a gallon of spring water for 3 minutes, then strain and allow to cool. Add to morning bathwater before heading out for the day.

## Super Power Good Luck Bath and Floor Wash for Business Success

Face east as the sun rises and say the Psalm 56 three times. Then add cinnamon, allspice, cloves and Hoyt's cologne to your bathwater. Pour over your head 9 times and say the 23rd Psalm 9 times. When you are done, allow yourself to air dry and dress in fresh clothes. Take a cupful of the bathwater to the eastern corner of your home and toss it in that direction, thanking the spirits for bringing you good luck.

Then make the following floor wash. To a bucket of hot water add 9 red pepper pods, 3 ounces of sugar, some ground nutmeg, and a little ammonia. Scrub your floor with that solution. Take some fast luck and add it to the water and scrub again. Always scrub going towards the back, never out the front door. Sweep the floor going from the front of the home to the back. Then say "May my crowd gather together thick. May my crowd gather together thick. May my crowd gather together thick. In the name of the Father, in the name of the Son, in the name of the Holy Spirit." Read the 47th Psalm and say "May my crowd gather together thick today, all gather together thick as hops, in the name of the Son and in the name of the Holy Spirit." That night, say the 56th Psalm 3 times.

You should have an unusually profitable day if you do this work correctly.

# Healing and Cleansing Spiritual Baths

## Basic Hoodoo Bath

Add a handful of salt and a little bluing to your bathwater for a quick cleansing. Works well for uncrossing, too.

## Bath for Healing a Head Cold

Add the following essential oils to a warm tub of water for relief from a head cold.

- Pine
- Cedar
- Camphor
- Menthol
- Spruce

## Bath to Improve Your Life

By the light of 3 fresh white candles, add the following to your bathwater:

- Sea salt
- Florida water
- 1 fresh parsley bundle
- 1 nutmeg
- 1 bay leaf
- 1 fresh rosemary bundle
- 1 fresh sage bundle
- 1 fresh mint bundle
- 3 white eggs

Light a good cleansing incense like camphor or sage. Bathe with the eggs, by carefully rubbing them over your entire body, taking care not to break them. Dry off with a clean white towel. Put on all white clothes. Place the eggs in a brown paper sack and put them outside, along with the 3 white candles. The next morning take the eggs to the crossroads and leave them along with 21 pieces of candy and 3 coconuts. Ask the Spirit of the Crossroads to remove the obstacles from your life.

## Caribbean Cleansing

Add the following ingredients to a warm tub of water. Take this bath on Sunday mornings for spiritual maintenance.

- White flower petals

- 9 whole nutmegs
- Coconut milk
- River water

## Cleansing Bath

Add the following ingredients to one gallon of boiling water. Allow to cool and add to bath to clear negative energies.

- 1 cup sea salt
- 9 lemons
- 1 cup white vinegar

## Coffee Bath

Add a pot of strong black coffee to your bathwater when you are feeling under the weather. Bathe for 9 minutes. Dispose of the bathwater at a crossroads.

## Cooling Anger Bath

Based on a New Orleans Hoodoo formula, this bath will help end fighting and restore peace in the home. When you are really angry, take this bath to get a cool head back. It is very calming.

- Wormwood

- Passion Flower
- ¼ cup honey
- ¼ cup brown sugar
- Damask rose attar
- Pennyroyal

Simmer the ingredients in a gallon of spring water on the stove for 3 minutes. Strain and add the water to your bathwater. Completely submerge your head 13 times and say the Prayer of St. Francis for Peace.

## *Prayer of St. Francis*

*Lord, make me an instrument of your peace.*
*Where there is hatred, let me sow love.*
*Where there is injury, pardon.*
*Where there is doubt, faith.*
*Where there is despair, hope.*
*Where there is darkness, light.*
*Where there is sadness, joy.*
*O Divine Master,*
*Grant that I may not so much seek to*
*Be consoled, as to console;*
*To be understood, as to understand;*
*To be loved, as to love.*
*For it is in giving that we receive.*
*It is in pardoning that we are pardoned,*
*and it is in dying that we are born to Eternal Life.*
*Amen.*

## Dream Bath

This bath is designed to relax you and promote psychic dreams and visions. For best results, drink a cup of this tea while bathing in the bath before bedtime.

- Rose petals
- Mugwort
- Peppermint
- Cinnamon
- Vanilla

Simmer the herbs in a gallon of rainwater on the stove for 3 minutes. Use spring water as a substitute of you do not have rain water on hand. Strain and add the water to your bathwater. Save a cup to drink and add honey. Do this ritual immediately prior to bedtime for optimal effects.

## Empowerment Bath

When you need a shot of courage and want to gain control over a situation or condition, take this bath and focus on what you need.

- Carnation
- Ginger
- Frankincense

- Sandalwood
- Myrrh

Simmer the ingredients in whatever form available in a gallon of spring water on the stove for 9 minutes. Allow to cool and strain. Add the empowering water to your bathwater and pour over your head nine times while reciting Psalm 23.

## Energy Bath

When you feel depleted and in need of replenishing your energy, take this bath. This is an ideal bath for when you are sick also, and does wonders after participating in a draining magic ritual.

- Orange essential oil
- Lime juice
- Lemon verbena herb

Simmer the ingredients along with a gallon of spring water on your stove for 3 minutes. Allow to cool and strain. Add the ingredients to your bathwater and pour over your head nine times while reciting Psalm 23.

## Eucalyptus Healing Bath

Eucalyptus is often used as a singular healing ingredient in New Orleans Hoodoo. To make this bath, add a handful of eucalyptus leaves and a few drops of the essential oil to your bathwater. Take a white candle and rub it over your body being sure to get the bottoms of your feet and the palms of your hands. If there is a particular place of your body in need of healing, spend extra time rubbing the candle there. Then light the candle and allow it to burn all the way down. The candle will absorb negative energy. Place the wax remains in a paper bag and throw them in the trash.

## General Well-being Bath

When you are feeling under the weather and lacking energy, try this simple bath.

- 1 whole box Arm and Hammer baking soda
- Bergamot essential oil
- Handful of salt

Throw the above ingredients in your bathwater and bathe in it. The wash your face in running water and allow it to air dry. You should feel better after doing this. If you don't feel better, repeat the procedure for 9 days in a row and you will experience relief. Be sure to thank the saints each day while bathing.

## *Thanksgiving Prayer*

*Dear God, Jesus, Mama Mary, St. Joseph, St. Philomena, thank you for this day.*

Make the sign of the cross and state your request.

## Green Tea Healing Bath

Simmer the green tea and herbs on the stove for 9 minutes. Strain and add the water to your bathwater for overall wellbeing.

- 2 green tea bags
- Vanilla
- Vetiver
- Lemon
- Patchouli
- Orange peel

## Peaceful Healing Bath

When you are in need of spiritual or physical rejuvenation, or when you need to restore a sense of peace and wellbeing, try the Peaceful Healing Bath.

- Fresh basil
- ¼ cup honey
- 3 cinnamon sticks

- Florida water
- Holy water
- 9 white carnations
- 1 cup coconut milk

Boil together 1 bunch of fresh basil, 1/4 cup honey and 3 cinnamon sticks for 9 minutes. Allow to cool. Strain into a large clean bowl. Add 3 splashes of Florida water, 3 splashes of holy water, the petals of 9 white carnations and 1 cup coconut milk. Pour into warm bath and soak until bath cools.

## Psychic Head Wash
Allow the following ingredients to sit in fresh water for 24 hours. Wash your head with the solutions to bring psychic enhancement.

- 3 cinnamon sticks
- Fresh thyme
- 3 nutmeg
- 3 bay leaves
- Lemon grass

## Purify the Soul
Take this bath when healing is needed.
- White carnations

- Cinnamon sticks
- Coconut water
- Holy water
- Goat's milk

Boil the cinnamon sticks in a gallon of water. Allow to cool and strain. Add the carnations, coconut water, holy water and goat's milk. This bath should be done before bed.

## Spiritual Cleansing Bath

To wash away evil messes and restore your spirit to a clean slate, try this bath.

- Holy water
- White flower petals
- Sea salt
- Epsom salt
- Baking soda
- Goat's milk
- 3 eggs

Add everything to bathwater. Rub yourself from head to foot with each egg. When you are done, dry off with a clean white towel. Place the eggs in a brown paper sack and remove to outside trash.

## Stone Bath

- White cloth
- White stone
- 4 white candles
- Sea salt

Place a new white cloth on the floor. Place a white, washed stone in the center of the cloth. Pour some sea salt on top of the stone. Place a white candle at the four corners of the cloth, light the candles and state your problems. Allow the candles to burn down. Tie up the white cloth and place the bundle in your bath. After bathing, untie the cloth and allow the salt to go out with the bathwater. Place the cloth in the trash and return the stone to nature.

# LGBT Baths

Of course any of the baths in this book can be used by anyone and most baths are not bound to opposite sex relationships. However, there are some that are formulated specifically for same sex couples such as the ones in this section.

## Attraction Bath

Simmer the following herbs for 9 minutes on the stove. Allow to cool and add to your bathwater. Burn some safflower petals on charcoal while bathing to amplify the attraction factor. Then go out on the town and see who comes your way!

- Catnip
- Violets
- Cubeb berries

## Dixie Love Bath

Take this bath when you need to have members of the same sex give in to your every whim. Works well with opposite sex couples also.

- Rose
- Gardenia
- Magnolia
- Patchouli
- Cinnamon
- Jasmine
- Lavender

Simmer the herbs for 9 minutes on the stove. Allow to cool and add to your bathwater. You may substitute essential oils for any of the herbs you may not have on hand.

## Dryad Conjure Bath

To attract and keep a lover, take this bath before an encounter. Add the essential oils to a base of almond oil for a potent conjure oil you can use to anoint a purple candle under which you place a written petition to protect and cherish a relationship.

- Lavender
- Musk
- Oakmoss
- Vanilla bean

Simmer the above herbs for 9 minutes on the stove. Allow to cool and add to your bathwater.

## Follow Me Boy

According to New Orleans legend, this recipe was created in the 1890s by Marie Laveau, the Voodoo Queen of New Orleans. Originally designed for prostitutes, this bath has money, love, and protection herbs incorporated in it. The recipe dates back almost 150 years. This bath is very effective for men wishing to attract other men.

- Orris root
- Dried Catnip
- Lavender
- Calamus
- Licorice
- Damiana
- Jasmine flowers
- Rose absolute
- Vanilla
- Night jasmine essential oil
- Piece of Queen Elizabeth root

Simmer the above herbs for 9 minutes on the stove. Allow to cool and add to your bathwater. You may substitute essential oils for any of the herbs you may not have on hand but if you do, add them once the solutions cools. Pour some of the water over your head 9 times and say the 23rd Psalm. Save a cup of the bathwater and take it to the crossroads and throw the water to the east. Walk home without looking back.

## Follow Me Girl

For the flip side of the *Follow Me Boy* coin, this bath is excellent for women wishing to attract other women.

- Myrrh resin
- Patchouli essential oil
- Vetivert herb
- Lemongrass herb
- Vanilla bean
- Sandalwood essential oil

Simmer the myrrh resin, vetivert, lemongrass and vanilla bean on the stove for 9 minutes. Strain and add to the bathwater. Add the essential oils last. Pour some of the water over your head 9 times and say the 23rd Psalm. Save a cup of the bathwater and take it to the crossroads and throw the water to the east. Walk home without looking back.

## Kiss Me Now

Try this bath to increase your seductive power and to have a good time with the partner of your choice.

- Narcissus
- Cassia
- Rose
- Citronella
- Lemongrass
- Musk

Simmer the herbs for 9 minutes on the stove. Allow to cool and add to your bathwater. Pour some of the water over your head 9 times and say the 23rd Psalm 9 times. Save a cup of the bathwater and take it to the crossroads and throw the water to the east. Walk home without looking back.

## Kundalini Bath

This bath is based on the formula for the conjure oil of the same name designed for women who wish to attract other women. Draw a warm bath and add the essential oils to the bathwater.

- Amber essential oil
- Rose essential oil
- Patchouli essential oil

## Lavender Lust Bath

Simmer the following herbs for 9 minutes on the stove. Allow to cool and add to your bathwater for a boost in libido.

- Lavender essential Oil
- Handful of fresh lavender (dried will do if you don't have fresh)
- Handful of violets or violet fragrance oil

## Q Bath

This bath is most often used by men seeking love and sex with other men. Guys swear by the effectiveness of this bath.

- Queen Elizabeth Root
- Handful of catnip

Simmer the above ingredients on the stove for 9 minutes, strain and add to your bathwater. Take the Queen Elizabeth root and allow it to dry out then anoint with a conjure oil specific to your purpose and carry it with you as your personal miracle worker.

## 3 Roots Nature Bath

When you have lost your nature and want it back. Simmer the following herbs for 9 minutes on the stove. Allow to cool and add to your bathwater.

- Burdock Root
- Queen Elizabeth Root
- High John the Conqueror Root

# Love Bath Recipes

## Adam and Eve Bath

Take an Adam and Eve Bath to help you find your soul mate and when you want to strengthen the love in a relationship. It is also excellent for drawing love bringing your lover back to you if you have drifted apart or fought. Use either the essential oils or the herbs for this bath – or a combination of both.

- Rose geranium
- Musk Oil
- Melissa
- Apple Blossom

## Chuparrosa Bath

This bath is used to attract love and excitement and to ensure that when you meet your desired partner, they will return your passion in full.

- Honeysuckle
- Rose
- Gardenia
- Honey

Use either the essential oils or the herbs for this bath – or a combination of both. Say the prayer to the Chuparrosa while relaxing in the tub.

### *Prayer to the Chuparrosa*

*"Divine Hummingbird, Who enriches and glorifies everything with your Holy Power, I ask that you enrich my life and love with your Divine Intercession so that my lover will want only me. In the same way that you extract honey from flowers, extract all misfortune and bad luck from my life; I pray you will not forget me, so that my lover and I may share a relationship that is honest and true."*

## Cleo May Bath

The Cleo May formula is based on an olde-time New Orleans recipe designed for prostitutes who sought to attract high end clientele with the ability to pay large sums of money. Today, Cleo May products are valued for their ability to promote the economic status of women and to draw men with means and are not used solely by prostitutes anymore. A Cleo May bath can be used by any woman interested in securing a sugar daddy.

- Jezebel root
- Magnolia blooms or fragrance oil
- Carnation flowers

- Rose petals
- Orange
- Vanilla
- Vetivert
- Almond oil

Use either the essential oils or the herbs for this bath – or a combination of both. Add to a warm bath and be sure to completely submerge yourself. You can also combine the ingredients in a bottle of almond oil for sensuous massage oil.

## Cleopatra Bath

An exotic bath unparalleled for invoking sexual possibilities into one's life.

- Lotus
- Sandalwood
- Ylang ylang
- Honeysuckle
- Orange
- 1 cup powdered milk

Use either the herbs or the essential oils or a combination of both. Add to the bathwater and say your prayers nine times.

## Come to Me

A bath designed to be used as a subtly coercive invitation to romance. Take this bath before going out on the town to attract the person of your desires.

- Rose petals
- Jasmine flowers
- Gardenia essential oil
- Lemon essential oil

## Dove's Blood

This is a good bath to take when healing from a broken heart and working out difficult problems in relationships. Brings happiness and joy where sorrow resided. Also works well as a protection and uncrossing bath.

- Dragon's blood oil
- Rose oil
- Cinnamon stick

## Love Bath

Tie the following herbs into a bundle and use in your bath on Fridays to draw love and romance to you. Alternately, you can simmer the herbs for three minutes on the stove to make a tea, allow to cool and add to the bathwater.

- Calamus root
- Jasmine flowers
- Dandelion root
- Lemon balm
- Rose petals
- Mint leaves
- Chamomile flowers

# Orisha Spiritual Bath Recipes

## Changó Cleansing Bath

Changó (Shango, Xango) is the orisha of lightening, dance, thunder, power, passion, and sensuality. He has the power to win wars, defeat enemies, and gain power over others. He will ensure victory over all difficulties. Chàngó is said to have once been a Yoruban king.

- Sarsaparilla
- Pomegranate juice
- Sea salt
- Cream
- Cascarilla

Boil the sarsaparilla in a gallon of water. Allow to cool. Add the rest of the ingredients and use in your bathwater for 3 nights in a row when you feel you are in extreme danger.

## Elegba Road Opener Bath

In Santería and Yoruban traditions, Ellegua is the Guardian of the Crossroads. He is petitioned to open doors to opportunities and to remove obstacles.

- Abre camino
- Fresh mint
- Guava juice
- Sweet basil
- Rum
- Florida water
- Holy water

Add all ingredients to a large glass bowl. Allow to sit for 3 days. Bathe with this on a Monday.

## Elegba Reverse Bad Luck Bath
To remove obstacles and reverse bad luck.

- Guava juice
- Saffron
- Sea salt
- Cascarilla
- Holy water
- Florida water
- White rum
- Reverse candle (white/black)

Bloom the saffron in warm water. Add the rest of the ingredients and allow to sit for 3 days with a reverse (black/white) candle. Bathe for 30 minutes for 3 nights with the candle burning.

## Obàtálá Cleansing Bath

Obàtálá is the creator orisha, a symbol of peace and purity, the Father of humankind, and messenger to Olofi, the ruler of the World. His color is white, containing all the colors of the rainbow. He rules the mind and intellect, male and female. Obàtálá is likened to the patron saint Our Lady of Mercy.

By the light of a white candle and in a clean space, mix together white flower petals, coconut water, cascarilla and Florida water. Add one gallon of fresh clear water. Use this bath on 4 Thursday's in a single month.

## Ogun Protection Bath

Ogun is a very powerful orisha. He is considered the Father of Technology and presides over fire, iron, hunting, politics and war. Take this bath when you need his protection.

- Plantain leaves
- Coconut water
- Cascarilla
- Florida water
- Leeks

Boil the plantain leaves and leeks in one gallon of water. Allow to cool and strain. Add remaining ingredients. This bath should be done for 3 days before having surgery.

## Oshun Blessing Bath

Oshun is an Orisha of love, intimacy, beauty, wealth and diplomacy. She is often petitioned for blessings and matters of the heart and finances. When in need of her blessings, add 5 whole oranges to your bath. Rub the oranges over your body. Afterwards, take the oranges to a river and offer them to Oshun.

*orange*
*water*
*5 drops essential oil, freeze dried orange slices*

## Oshun Love Bath

Mix together 5 cinnamon sticks, 5 tablespoons of honey, petals from 5 yellow flowers, 5 tablespoons champagne and 5 drops of good perfume in a large copper bowl. Add to your bathwater for 5 nights in a row asking Oshun to bring you love.

## Oshun Money Bath

To bring money to you.

- Champagne
- Mint

- Brown mustard seeds
- Cinnamon sticks
- Florida water

Boil the mustard seeds, mint and cinnamon sticks for 5 minutes. Allow to cool and strain. Add to your bathwater along with the champagne and Florida water. This bath gets fast results.

## Oshun Seduction Bath

To draw passion to you and increase your seductive power, try this bath.

- Cinnamon sticks
- Cream
- Brown sugar
- Romaine lettuce
- Honey
- Perfume

Boil the cinnamon sticks, honey and brown sugar. Allow to cool and strain. Add the remaining ingredients. Allow to sit for 5 minutes. Add to bathwater.

## Oyá Power Bath

Oyá provides protection from the elements, strong winds, and hurricanes. She is the orisha to summon for help in business and prosperity in economic affairs. She also provides protection for ancestral spirits and rules the cemeteries.

- Cemetery flowers
- Eggplant
- Rain water
- Pomegranate juice

Boil the cemetery flowers and eggplant in one gallon of water for 9 minutes. Allow to cool and strain. Add the rain water and pomegranate juice. Add to bathwater when working with spirits.

## Yemayá Tranquility Bath

Yemayá is the Mother of the Seven Seas, the Santería orisha of fertility and motherhood. She offers protection to women. She is likened to the patron saints Lady of Regla, and Mary, Star of the Sea.

- Basil
- Cascarilla
- Sea water
- Florida water

- Coconut water
- Watermelon

When in need of calm and peace take this spiritual bath. Add all ingredients to a large bowl. Allow to sit for 7 minutes. Strain and add to bathwater.

## Yemayá Protection Bath
For protection from the Mother of all orishas.

- Watercress
- Mint
- Sea water
- Coconut water

Cut the watercress and mint into fine pieces. Add sea water and coconut water. This bath should be done for 7 days.

## Seven African Powers Bath (1)
This spiritual bath calls on the blessings of the Seven African Powers to bring success, protection, luck, love, and money.

- Abre camino herb
- Gardenia flowers

- Violets
- Rosemary
- Peppermint
- Anise
- ¼ cup brown sugar
- 1 cup Florida Water

Simmer the above ingredients for 9 minutes on the stove. Allow to cool and add to your bathwater.

## Seven African Powers Bath (2)

This Seven African Powers bath is for power and protection.

- 7 multi colored roses
- Holy water
- Coconut water
- Ache de Santo
- Rain water
- Orange water

Boil the ache de Santo in one gallon of water. Allow to cool. Take the rose petals and cut them into tiny pieces. Place in a large clean glass bowl. Add holy water and coconut water. Add cooled ache de Santo liquid. Add to bathwater and bathe for 30 minutes when power and protection is needed.

## Seven African Powers Bath (3)

This bath is when you have special needs and are
asking for favors from the orishas.

- Mint
- Rose petals
- Rosemary
- Violet water
- Sea water
- River water
- Coconut water
- Florida water
- Palm oil
- Cascarilla

Boil the rosemary, mint and palm oil in a gallon of
water. Allow it to cool and strain. Cut the rose petals
into small pieces. Add the rest of the ingredients.
Bathe in this when asking for favors and special
requests.

# Planetary Baths

The baths that follow are based on planetary formulas in the Goetic magic tradition. Take one of these baths prior to performing a Goetic ritual for amplifying ideal conditions for summoning spirits. The herbs listed for each of the baths correspond to the herbal formulations of the planetary incenses, so you can combine the herbs and burn them as incense during rituals or even in combination with your bath to enhance the effects.

## Earth Bath
Add the following herbs to a gallon of spring water and allow it to simmer for 9 minutes. Strain and add to your bathwater for amplifying Earth's qualities in your life.

- Sage
- Elder pith

## Jupiter Bath
Simmer the above herbs for 9 minutes on the stove. Allow the solution to cool, and then add to your bathwater. Add the food coloring directly to the bathwater.

- Saffron
- Linseed
- Violet roots
- Peony blossoms
- Betony leaves
- Birch leaves
- Blue food coloring

## Mars Bath

Simmer the following ingredients for 9 minutes on the stove. Allow the solution to cool and add to your bathwater. Add food coloring directly to the bathwater.

- Myrrh
- Storax
- Benzoin
- Aloes wood
- Red and blue food coloring (to make purple)

## Mercury Bath

Simmer the following ingredients for 9 minutes on the stove. Allow the solution to cool and add to your bathwater. Add the food coloring directly to the bathwater.

- Mastic
- Carnation blossoms
- Aniseed
- Juniper wood
- Chamomile blossoms
- Valerian roots
- Red and yellow food coloring (to make orange)

## Moon Bath

Add the following herbs to a gallon of spring water and allow it to simmer for 9 minutes. Strain and add to your bathwater for amplifying Moon's qualities in your life.

- Aloes Wood
- Benzoin
- Camphor

## Saturn Bath

Simmer the following ingredients for 9 minutes on the stove. Allow the solution to cool and add to your bathwater. Add the food coloring directly to the bathwater.

- Black poppy seeds

- Willow leaves
- Rue leaves
- Fern
- Cumin
- Fennel seeds
- Blue and red food coloring (to make purple)

## Sun Bath

Add the following herbs to a gallon of spring water and allow the solution to simmer for 9 minutes. Strain and add to your bathwater for amplifying the Sun's qualities in your life.

- Sandalwood essential oil
- Myrrh essential oil
- Aloes wood powder or pieces
- Saffron herb
- Carnation blossoms
- Laurel leaves

## Venus Bath

Simmer the following ingredients for 9 minutes on the stove. Allow the solution to cool and add to your bathwater. Add the food coloring directly to the bathwater.

- Cinnamon stick
- Rose blossoms
- Coriander seeds
- Lilly of the valley oil
- Green food coloring

# Protection Baths

## Ammonia Bath

The most basic of protection and uncrossing baths in the old time Hoodoo tradition consists of ¼ cup of ammonia added to bathwater. Take this bath for 9 days. Keep your Bible next to the tub and read the 45th and 54th psalms while bathing. Take a cupful of bathwater when you are finished to the east corner of your home and toss it in that direction while saying the *Glory Be* prayer.

### *Glory Be*

*Glory to the Father and to the Son and to the Holy Spirit, As it was in the beginning, is now and ever shall be, world without end. Amen.*

## Dragon's Blood Bath

Next to High John, this bath is the most positive and protective.

- Dragon's Blood (you can use the chunks here but it will stain your bath tub so you will have to bleach it out. The alternative is to use Dragon's Blood oil)

- Cinnamon
- Vetivert

Simmer the above ingredients for 9 minutes on the stove. Allow to cool and add to your bathwater. Pour some of the bathwater over your head 9 times and say the *Prayer to St. Benedict* 9 times.

### *Prayer to St. Benedict*
*God our Father you made St. Benedict As an outstanding guide to teach man and woman how to live in your service. Grant by preparing your love to one another that we may walk in the way of your commandments to Christ our lord. Amen.*

## Fiery Wall of Protection Bath
Fiery Wall of Protection is New Orleans' best-known protection formula. Used in a protection bath, it squashes any type of threat or threatening condition, whether it be a psychic or spiritual attack, or more mundane legal, health and business issues.

- Frankincense essential oil
- Dragon's Blood conjure oil
- Handful of Rue
- Handful of blessed salt
- Ginger essential oil

- 3 bay leaves

Make a tea from the rue and the bay leaves by simmering the herbs on the stove for three minutes. Strain and add to the bathwater. Add the oils. Pour some of the bathwater over your head 9 times and say the *Prayer to St. Michael* 9 times. When you are done, take some of the bathwater and toss to the east while thanking the spirits for their protection.

### Prayer to St. Michael
*Saint Michael the Archangel, defend us in battle; be our protection against the wickedness and snares of the devil. May God rebuke him, we humbly pray, and do thou, O Prince of the heavenly host, by the power of God, thrust into hell Satan and all the evil spirits who prowl about the world seeking the ruin of souls. Amen.*

## High John the Conqueror Bath
For the highest protection and removal of negative energies while adding the most positive blessings, take this High John the Conqueror bath.

- High John the Conqueror Root
- Cedarwood
- Vetivert

Simmer the above ingredients on the stove for 9 minutes. Strain and add to the bathwater. Pour some of the water over your head 9 times and say the *Prayer to High John the Conqueror* 9 times. Carry the High John root with you for ongoing protection.

## *Prayer to High John the Conqueror*
*May the Almighty and All Powerful on High, the Soul of John the Conqueror, watch over me and show me the way to defeat my problems, to overcome fear and conquer my enemies, and to achieve the magnificent goals of my dreams and desires. Amen.*

# Spiritual Waters

## Angel Water (Eau'd Ange)

Angel Water, also called *Portugal Water*, is said to have its roots in Portugal. It first made its appearance in hoodoo during the eighteenth century.

- Rose water
- Orange water
- Myrtle water
- Amber oil
- Musk Oil
- ½ dram of violet, rose, or verbena essential oil

Agitate the ingredients together in a bottle briskly for some hours. Do this frequently for a few days, keeping the bottle (closely stopped) in a warm room. After repose, decant the clear portion, and if necessary, filter the fluid through white bibulous paper. The mixture should be nearly colorless.[1] Almost miraculous virtues are attributed to this delicious water. Add 1 cup to your bathwater for a

---

[1] *The Scientific American Cyclopedia of Receipts, Notes and Queries* edited by Albert Allis Hopkins, 1901.

sensual bath and when in need of blessings of your guardian angel.

## Anise Spirit Water (Eau Spiritueuse d' Anis)

This traditional water is used for ancestral works, for summoning spirits of the dead, and in Spiritualist work such as when performing séances. Here is the original formula and proportions.

- 16 ounces angelica seed
- 6 ounces anise
- 8 pounds brandy

Bruise the seeds, and combine with the brandy for a few days, taking care to gently swirl the solution daily. Add to distilled water to dilute. The resulting liquid will be cloudy upon blending the water and alcohol. Add a cupful to your bathwater before functioning as a medium and before séances and misas.

## Creole Water

This is traditional spiritual water that can be used when working with New Orleans-specific spirits.

- 6¾ ounces orris root
- 1½ pints French brandy
- 3 drams oil of orange blossoms
- ¾ fluid ounce oil of geranium
- Essence of cumerin

Cut the orris root into small pieces and add to the French brandy. Allow to sit for two weeks, gently swirling the mixture daily. After two weeks, you can either strain the brandy or keep the orris root pieces in the brandy—I like to keep the herbal matter in my mother oils and waters, but this is a matter of personal preference. Then, add the oil of orange blossoms and the oil of geranium. Finally, add the essence of cumerin—the amount is up to you, and depends on how you want the final product to smell. Add a cupful of Creole water to your bathwater prior to calling upon the New Orleans spirits.

## Herb Water

Herb waters are great to keep in the fridge for about a week. You can make herb water with basil, mint, parsley, rosemary, thyme or sage. Place herbs in one gallon of water. Simmer for 30 minutes. Allow to cool. Squeeze the herbs and remove. Strain the water. Add 3 tablespoons vodka or white rum. Add 1 cup to bathwater for overall healing and wellbeing.

## Hoyt's Cologne

One of the most popular of the cologne waters for drawing luck in games of chance is *Hoyt's Cologne*. It is often added to floor washes and bathwater for good luck. While the exact proprietary blend is unknown, there are some close approximations. Following is one such formula according to the *American Pharmaceutical and Druggist Record*, Volume 33.

- 1 dram oil of rose geranium
- 2 drams oil of lemon
- 30 mm oil of patchouli
- 1½ ounces oil of bergamot
- 2 drams oil of lemon
- 4 drams oil of lavender
- 60 mms oil of sandalwood
- 60 mms oil of snakeroot
- 30 mms oil of neroli
- 1 ounce tincture of storax
- 1½ ounces extract of orris root (fluid)
- 12 grams musk
- 30 fluid ounces alcohol

Combine the above ingredients and let sit for sixty days, shaking the solution daily. The result resembles Hoyt's Cologne.[2]

## Hungary Water

Also called *Compound Spirit of Rosemary* or *Eau d' Hongrie*. Add Hungary water to your bathwater as a magickal aid for women in need of empowerment. It can also be worn as cologne or sprayed about the home for protection, to ward off evil, and to bring good luck to family matters.

- 2 pounds rosemary tops in blossom
- ¼ pound fresh sage
- 3 quarts grain alcohol
- 1 quart distilled water
- ½ pound table salt
- 1 ounce Jamaican ginger (bruised)

Combine all ingredients except for the distilled water and Jamaica ginger. Let sit for a few days and either decant or filter the plant matter from the liquid. Add the distilled water and then the Jamaica ginger.

---

[2] *American Pharmaceutical and Druggist Record*, Vol. 33, American Druggist Publishing Co., 1898.

## Jockey Club

Jockey Club is unquestionably the most famous New Orleans gambling cologne. Its origin actually lies with the famous French perfumer, Jean-Baptiste Rigaud.

- 1 pint extract of jasmine
- ¾ pint tincture of ambergris
- 1 ½ pints extract of rose
- ¾ pint extract of tuberose
- 3 pints tincture of orris root
- 1 ½ pints essence of rose (triple)
- ¾ ounce oil of bergamot

Use the above ingredients in the strength that suits you. Mix with distilled water to make wonderful cologne and add to your bathwater before gambling.

## Kananga Water

Charmed by the mysterious legend of the Kananga flower (ylang ylang) of Japan, Jean-Baptiste Rigaud created *Eau de Kananga* in 1869 and it quickly became a great sensation throughout Europe and the United States.

- 10 minims oil of ylang ylang
- 5 minims oil of neroli
- 5 minims oil of rose

- 3 minims oil of bergamot
- 10 ounces alcohol
- One grain of musk (optional)

Dilute with distilled water to make a toilet water.[3] Add to your bathwater for blessings and to increase fertility.

## La Santísima Muerte Water

Gather 21 fresh flowers from a cemetery in the moonlight. Bring 1 gallon of holy water to a boil. Pour over cemetery flowers in a glass bowl. Cover with a clean white cloth and allow to sit for 24 hours. Then place in refrigerator for 3 days. After 3 days, strain and add 1 cup white rum or tequila. Pour into a clean glass jar. Add 1/2 cup to bathwater before working with La Santísima Muerte.

## Notre Dame Water

Water of Notre Dame can be sprayed about the home to make peace and bring blessings. It can also be used to in spells to summon spirits, cleansing spells and

[3] *Manual of Formulas, Recipes, Methods, and Secret Processes* edited by Raymond B. Wailes, Popular Science Publishing Co., New York, 1932.

baths, and uncrossings works and baths. Add 1 cup to your bathwater.

- Holy water
- White rosewater
- Violet hydrosol
- Little John the Conqueror root

Mix the above ingredients and add to a spray bottle and bathwater. Keep the bottle on your altar or on or near your Bible.

## Sea Water

Some conjure works in the South call for salt water, which is readily available in the Gulf of Mexico. If you do not live close to the sea, here is a recipe for sea water that so closely resembles actual sea water that it will actually support marine life in an aquarium.[4]

- 81 grams table salt
- 7 grams Epsom salts
- 10 grams magnesium chloride
- 2 grams potassium chloride
- 3 to 4 liters of water

---

[4] The Scientific American Cyclopedia of Receipts, Notes and Queries edited by Albert Allis Hopkins, 1901.

## Violet Water

Pour boiling water over fresh violets in a clean glass bowl. Cover and steep for 24 hours. Place in the fridge for 2 or 3 days. Strain and add 2 tablespoons of vodka. African violets and roses can be prepared in this way, as well. Use this water to spritz around the home to promote peace and love. Add to baths when relationships need soothing and to foster peace within you.

# Uncrossing Baths

## Hoodoo Uncrossing Bath

To wash off bad luck and put on good luck, take this Hoodoo Uncrossing bath by adding the ingredients to your bathwater.

- Bluestone
- Saltpeter
- Sugar
- alum

Mix the bath in a basin and stand in your tub for this one. Pour the water over your head 9 times and say Psalm 37 each time for a total of 9 times.

## La Madama Uncrossing Bath

La Madama is a great protector. This bath was given to Madrina in a dream. It's an all round good bath for whatever ails you. Add ingredients to your bathwater.

- 1 cup apple cider vinegar
- 3 tablespoons sea salt
- 1 silver dime

This bath should be done on a Saturday.

## Spiritual Power Bath

Use this bath to remove heavy, negative influences. Place all ingredients in a large clean glass bowl. Allow to sit for 24 hours. Strain and add 3 tablespoons of clear white rum.

- Florida water
- Violet water
- Holy water
- River water
- Rain water
- Sea salt
- Coconut water
- Cascarilla
- Cedar chips
- Sage
- Grain of paradise
- 1 wish bone

## Super Uncrossing Bath

When you feel you are under spiritual attack, boost your defenses with this Super Uncrossing Bath.

Simmer the ingredients for 9 minutes on the stove. Allow to cool and add to your bathwater.

- Laundry bluing
- Basil
- Fennel
- Dill
- Rosemary
- Bay leaves
- Sea salt
- Epsom salt

## Uncrossing Bath

- White roses
- Bay leaf
- Fresh lavender
- Rain water
- Pinch of red brick dust

Boil the roses, red brick dust and bay leaf for 30 minutes in a gallon of spring water. Allow to cool and strain. Add fresh lavender and rain water. Add to bath for 3 nights. You can say Psalm 37 when taking this bath for added insurance.

# Wealth and Prosperity Baths

## Bring Me Money Bath

- Fresh basil
- 3 oranges
- Golden seal
- 3 bay leaves

Boil the golden seal and bay leaves in one gallon of water. Allow to cool and strain. Add fresh basil. Allow to sit for 3 hours. Strain again. Pour into your bath. Add the oranges and bathe with them until bath cools. Remove the oranges to the trash and take some of the bathwater to the crossroads.

## Easy Money Bath
Take this bath regularly to remove obstacles to financial freedom and to draw money to you.

- Cinnamon essential oil
- Patchouli essential oil
- 1 magnet

Add the above ingredients to your bathwater. Submerge completely 7 times. When done, keep the magnet in your wallet to keep attracting money.

## Fast Luck Bath

This Fast Luck Bath is a mixture of 9 essential oils and is used for business success.

- Cinnamon essential oil
- Wintergreen essential oil
- Geranium essential oil
- Bergamot essential oil
- Orange flowers essential oil
- Lavender essential oil
- Anise essential oil
- St. Michael conjure oil
- Rosemary essential oil

Add all of the essential oils to a warm tub of bath. Soak for a few minutes and completely submerge, then stand in the tub and rub the bathwater upwards on your body. Air dry. When done, save the bathwater and use as a floor wash in your home or business.

## Has No Hannah Gambling Bath

Take this gambling bath before playing games of
chance to get the edge.

- Jasmine essential oil
- Cinnamon essential oil
- Handful of mint

## Midnight Money Bath

- Chamomile flowers
- Flax seeds
- Fresh rain water

At 6 am tie the flax seeds in a green cloth. Place in a
clean glass bowl. Add chamomile flowers. Pour fresh
rain water over until covered. Allow to sit until
midnight. Add to your bath. Soak for 30 minutes.

## Money Bath

Add the following ingredients to your bathwater.
Take this bath 3 times per week to keep money
flowing in.

- Goats milk
- 2 Loadstones

- 9 pennies
- 3 vanilla beans

## Sweet Money Bath

Boil the following ingredients in a gallon of water. Allow to cool and strain. Add to your bathwater when you need to draw money fast.

- Nutmeg
- Irish moss
- Candied ginger
- Brown sugar
- Honey
- Sweet basil

## Wealth Drawing Bath

Add the following ingredients to bath nightly to attract and keep wealth.

- Brown sugar
- Laundry bluing
- Fresh basil

## To Attract Money

To attract money, bathe yourself in the morning

before sunrise in a bath with the above ingredients added.

- 1 cup of cow's milk
- 1 cup of goat's milk
- 1 cup of coconut milk
- 1 bottle of Florida water
- 1 cup of honey

## Weekly Wealth Bath

Bathe with the above combined ingredients to insure wealth comes your way. Keep the coins in your pocket or wallet. Reuse coins in your bathwater weekly.

- 3 gold coins
- Irish moss
- Bay leaf
- Chamomile flowers
- alfalfa

## Willie Mae's Mo' Money Bath

Boil the following ingredients in one gallon of water. Allow to cool. Strain and use for 3 baths.

- Nutmeg

- Cedar chips
- Parsley
- Galangal root
- Snake root
- 3 dimes

# Wisdom and Personal Mastery Baths

## Clarity Bath (1)

For clarity of thought and sound decision-making, bathe yourself in a bath with the following ingredients added in the morning before sunrise.

- Orange
- Sage
- Solomon's Seal
- Lavender
- Bay Rum
- Coconut milk

## Clarity Bath (2)

Grate a fresh coconut into a clean glass bowl. Add holy water, Florida water and cascarilla. This bath should be taken for 3 days in a row.

## Concentration Bath

To improve concentration, add the following essential oils to your bathwater before studying or whenever you need focus and concentration.

- Cedarwood
- Sandalwood
- Melissa
- Blue cypress
- Lavender
- Orange

## Crossroads Bath

When you need to get clarity on a situation and make a good decision, and to open roads and keep enemies out of the picture, take this Crossroads Bath.

- Pebble from a crossroads
- 1.8 cup of avocado oil
- 1 cup coconut milk
- ½ cup of strong coffee
- Pinch of brown sugar
- ¼ cup rum
- Bay leaf

Add the ingredients to your bathwater. Say the *Road Opener Prayer* three times while pouring some of the bathwater over your head three times. Save some of the water when you are done and dispose of at a crossroads.

### *Road Opener Prayer*

*God before me*
*God behind me*
*I on Thy path, O God*
*Thou, O God, in my steps.*
*In the twistings of the road.*
*In the currents of the river.*
*Be with me by day.*
*Be with me by night.*
*Be with me by day and*
*by night.*

## King Solomon Wisdom Bath

To improve decision-making, and increase mental powers take the following bath. This bath is also ideal for taking prior to studying and test-taking.

- Solomon's seal
- High John the Conqueror root
- Master root
- Bay leaf
- Goldenseal root
- Licorice root

Add the ingredients to a gallon of water and bring to a boil. Simmer for 9 minutes and allow to cool. Add to the bathwater and pour over your head nine times. Say the following King Solomon prayer 9 times:

*Give me wisdom and knowledge as that which was bestowed upon King Solomon, may all my works be crowned with success, now. In the name of the Father, the Son and the Holy Ghost. Amen.*

## Master Bath

Boil the following ingredients in a gallon of water. Allow to cool and strain. Add to your bathwater when you want to sharpen your mental acuity or before a test or situation that requires thinking on your toes.

- Master root
- Galangal
- Myrrh
- Mimosa
- Patchouli

## Master Key Bath

Boil the following ingredients in a gallon of water. Allow to cool, strain and add to your bathwater.

- Master root
- Myrrh essential oil
- Jasmine flowers
- Cinnamon stick

## Mastery and Influence Bath

To improve leadership qualities and self esteem, increase personal power and influence over others add the following to your bathwater.

- Coriander seeds
- Licorice root
- Sweet flag
- Laundry bluing

# Lagniappe

Lagniappe is a colloquial term used in New Orleans meaning "a little something extra." It is a true gesture of southern hospitality to throw in a little more of whatever it is a person is serving or selling to show sincere appreciation. It is in this spirit that we offer you a little lagniappe here.

## New Orleans Protection Bath

To keep evil at bay, enemies away and for protection, take this bath from the New Orleans Hoodoo tradition. Take a tablespoon of ammonia, a tablespoon of salt, and a tablespoon of vinegar and add it to your bath water nine days in a row. Bathe in this solution and pray Psalm 37 for protection from evil doers and crossings. For added protection, take some of your bath water each day and add some Van Van oil to it. Use as a floor wash to cleanse your home.

# Resources

**1) Planet Voodoo** - For authentic New Orleans Voodoo, hoodoo, conjure and rootwork supplies and services: altar dolls, conjure oils, herbs and roots, gris gris, curios, floor washes, spiritual waters, incense, jewelry, ju ju, sachet powders, spirit bottles, voodoo dolls, wanga pakets, doll babies, and zombies. www.planetvoodoo.com

**2) Root Mama Conjure** - Offering the finest in authentic occult items all handcrafted within the boundaries of sacred ritual for the modern world. All items are handcrafted within sacred space dedicated to bringing unique and powerful tools for the experienced and beginning practitioner. In true Hoodoo fashion, most items by are crafted using found, natural and recycled items making them unique and one of a kind.
www. rootmamaconjure.com

**3) Crossroads Mojo** - For all things related to crossroads conjure and more! Poppets and doll babies, conjure oils, jewelry and fetishes. www.crossroadsmojo.com

**4) Medicines and Curios** - complete inventory of spiritual supplies, old-fashioned remedies, curios,

botanicals, magickal oils, herbs, candles, sachet powders, spiritual baths and more!
www.medicinesandcurios.com

5) **Crossroads University** - The mission of Crossroads University is to preserve the integrity of traditional indigenous magical and spiritual technologies and healing systems and conserve the diverse cultural heritage of the American South. Specifically, we focus on the preservation of New Orleans Voodoo, Hoodoo, conjure, rootwork and root doctoring, and reinforce traditional methods of learning combined with contemporary technology of knowledge transmission for an enhanced learning experience of our students. Open enrollment.
www.crossroadsuniversity.com

6) **Planet Voodoo's Conjure Corner** – The forum and virtual campus for Crossroads University. Learn all about New Orleans Voodoo and Hoodoo and southern conjure. One need not be a student to join. Warm, friendly and nonjudgmental atmosphere!
www.conjurecorner.com

# About the Authors

**Denise Alvarado** is a native Creole born and raised in the Voodoo and hoodoo rich culture of New Orleans, Louisiana. She is an artist, independent researcher, and the author of several books, including the *Voodoo Hoodoo Spellbook, Voodoo Dolls in Magick and Ritual, the Voodoo Doll Spellbook* and *Hoodoo Almanac 2012,* coauthored with Carolina Dean and Alyne Pustanio. Denise is a rootworker in the southern hoodoo tradition, the founder and Editor in Chief of Hoodoo and Conjure Magazine and owner of Creole Moon Publications.

**Madrina Angelique** was born and raised in rural Georgia. She has immersed herself in the study and practice of traditional southern hoodoo since childhood. She is initiated in the Palo tradition as Madre Nganga of Munanso Centella Ndoki Nkuyo Malongo Corta Lima Cordosa, initiated by Chief Ololele Afolabi, godson of Tata Antonio Ali. She is also initiated in Santeria as Iyalorisha of Ile Ori Yemaya, initiated by Baba Ogun Solu, godson of Chief Bolu Fantunmise of the Ifa Orisha Cultural Center in Nigeria and Atlanta. Madrina is a regular contributor to Hoodoo and Conjure Magazine and coauthor of *13 Legendary Crossroads Rituals* with Denise Alvarado.

# To Our Readers

Creole Moon Publications is a small independent publisher specializing in the cultural and spiritual traditions and folklore of the American South. Our mission is to publish quality books that observe and preserve southern cultural heritage and folk magic traditions that will enrich people's lives.

Our readers are our most important resource, and we appreciate your input, suggestions, and ideas about what you would like to see published.

Visit our website at *www.creolemoon.com* to learn about our upcoming books and downloads, and to sign up for newsletters and exclusive offers.

You can also contact us at
creolemoon@planetvoodoo.com or at

Creole Moon Publications
P.O. Box 25687
Prescott Valley, AZ. 86312

Made in the USA
Monee, IL
03 November 2020